Note to grown-ups:
What 50 Things to do Before You're 11 ¾ is all about

The Great Outdoors holds boundless opportunities: to create, to learn, to walk and run, and to spend precious time with family and friends. Memories that last a lifetime are made through these experiences. And that's what **50 Things to do Before You're 11¾** is all about.

50 Things is a nationwide National Trust campaign to encourage children to take to the outdoors and enjoy classic adventures, from skimming stones to building dens.

We launched it in response to our Natural Childhood report, which highlighted research that fewer than one in ten children regularly play in wild places compared to almost half a generation ago, one-third have never climbed a tree, one in ten can't ride a bike, and three times as many are taken to hospital after falling out of bed as falling out of a tree.

Does this matter?
We think so.

On the one hand, our children no longer experience the wonders of nature and the chance to explore, face challenges and learn from them. Being stuck indoors can never provide the lasting memories, emotional connections or sense of reward from challenges overcome or imaginations fired up through playing outdoors.

On the other hand, some profound social problems are developing, storing up difficulties for the future. Three-tenths of children aged from two to fifteen are overweight or obese. One-tenth of five- to sixteen-year-olds have been diagnosed with a mental health problem. There are rising incidences of childhood asthma and noticeable declines in children's heart and lung fitness.

We do not know the cause of all these symptoms, but it is clear that access to nature and to exercise in fresh air can contribute to the solution. Their positive effect on physical and mental health, as well as to educational achievement, is well documented.

We hope that encouraging kids to get outdoors and try the 50 things will inspire them to create their own lifelong bond with nature. We want to give them back the chance to develop their own personal connection with the Great Outdoors – even if that means (calculated!) risk.

How to use this book

This book sets out the 50 best possible things to do before you're 11¾, along with other fun things to do outdoors – at the seaside, in the rain, across the seasons and even in your own garden!

Children matter to the National Trust, so we recommend that all activities within this book are supervised by an adult. We trust that you will make your own judgement about what is safe and suitable for the ability of your child. Just remember to have fun!

To make it extra easy to get involved, we've designed a brilliant website to help you plan where and when to do the activities and record your progress.

The 50 Things website

Sign up online at www.nationaltrust.org.uk/50things to meet your very own Outdoor Explorer, who will motivate your kids to get up and get outdoors. Your kids can personalise how their virtual explorer looks by doing the 'things' and winning rewards – there are even a few games for the best explorers.

The website also gives you and your family tips on how to get even better at these awesome adventures, and how to become a 50 Things expert.

So get outdoors and enjoy the world of adventure that awaits you!

Helen Meech
National Trust

01 Climb a tree

Choose one with sturdy branches from the bottom to the top.
Check out the view!

What you need:
- A tree with big strong branches you can reach from the ground
- Trainers or boots – leave your flip-flops behind
- A wave for everyone left down below

Top tip for success:
Keep three of your arms and legs on the tree at all times.

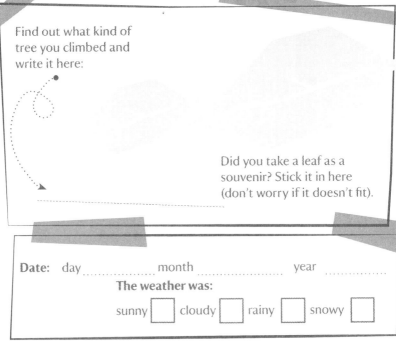

Find out what kind of tree you climbed and write it here:

Did you take a leaf as a souvenir? Stick it in here (don't worry if it doesn't fit).

Date: day .... month .... year ....

The weather was:

sunny ☐ cloudy ☐ rainy ☐ snowy ☐

Roll down a really big hill 02

It's the fun way to get to the bottom.

What you need:
- A grassy hill
- A clear run with nothing you might bump into

Top tip for success:
A fun roll is a fast roll. To really pick up speed lie on the grass, make your body into the shape of a sausage and roll down the hill sideways. Watch out for poo from animals like sheep, it can spread nasty germs!

Stick in a picture of you rolling down the hill:

How many times did you roll over?

Date: day .... month .... year ....

The weather was:

sunny ☐ cloudy ☐ rainy ☐ snowy ☐

03 Camp out in the wild

Why sleep in a boring old bed when you can sleep outside like a cowboy?

What you need:
- Go back to basics with a tent, ground mat and sleeping bag...or make yourself really cosy with your favourite pillow, duvet and a blow-up mattress
- Either way, everyone needs a torch

Top tip for success:
Before setting up your tent, pick a nice flat open area and clear away any stones or branches that might wake you up if you roll onto them.

My camping experience:

When I went to bed, I:
[tick boxes]

☐ Slept like a log

☐ Unzipped the tent and looked at the stars

☐ Wore an extra pair of socks

☐ Felt too excited to sleep

I heard:
- birds
- the wind
- the rain
- someone snoring very loudly

8

Pitching a tent
- Practise putting up your tent before you go away.
- Only pack what you need – roughing it is all part of the fun.
- Unpack the equipment and lay everything out neatly; have the instructions handy.
- Face the tent opening away from the direction of the wind.
- Don't store food in your tent as it will attract bugs and beasts – keep it in the car.

Look and listen
- Listen to the sounds of nature: the night cries of birds, the calls of foxes, the snuffles of hedgehogs and badgers, and the rustling of insects as they go about their business.
- When you leave, make sure you clear up all your litter.

Date: day .... month .... year ....
The weather was:
sunny ☐ cloudy ☐ rainy ☐ snowy ☐

04 Build a den

Branches, twigs and leaves make surprisingly cosy dens.

What you need:
- Branches, twigs, leaves and mud, all of which are generously provided by nature for free
- Leave the power tools at home, you won't need them here

Top tip for success:
Choose a dry, flat spot for the most solid den and never build with sharp objects. It could help to start by leaning sticks against a low tree branch like a wig-wam.

Make a list of all the things you used as building materials:

Draw the next den you plan to build:

Build a wigwam with bamboo canes, branches or old tent poles, or use a tree to support it on one side. Pack your structure with small branches or twigs, using lots of string or rope. Cover the outside with a large cloth to make your den waterproof – an old ground sheet is ideal. Fallen leaves will help keep the rain out, but you'll need lots of them. Make a soft carpet of old dried leaves or grass inside the den.

- Only use found materials to build your den – don't pull up or cut any living plants or trees.
- Don't use anything that is too big or too heavy – just in case it falls on top of you and hurts you.
- Take care not to poke yourself in the eye with pointy twigs or the tips of bamboo canes.
- Respect the environment – don't damage the site or leave any litter behind you.

Date: day .... month .... year ....
The weather was:
sunny ☐ cloudy ☐ rainy ☐ snowy ☐

05 Skim a stone

Can you do four bounces?

What you need:
- Flat water, like a lake or the sea on a calm day
- Somewhere to stand where you won't fall in when you throw really hard
- Some flat stones from near the water's edge

Top tip for success:
Choose your stone carefully: the smoother, rounder and flatter the better. Throw it hard and low so it spins quickly across the top of the water. Make sure there is nothing in the water that you might hit (like ducks or swimmers!).

Skimming score sheet

Player 1	Bounces	Player 2	Bounces
Throw 1		Throw 1	
Throw 2		Throw 2	
Throw 3		Throw 3	
Throw 4		Throw 4	
Throw 5		Throw 5	
Total		Total	

Date: day .... month .... year ....

The weather was:

sunny ☐ cloudy ☐ rainy ☐ snowy ☐

Don't forget to wear your wellies so you can make a splash!

What you need:
- A rainy day
- Welly boots
- A raincoat
- Or a towel and a change of clothes

Top tip for success:
Getting wet in the rain is only fun if you know you can soon get dry again. If you don't have a raincoat just dry off with a towel and change into some dry clothes.

Not everybody likes getting wet but some animals love it!
Make a list of all the animals you think might be happy when it rains:

....

....

....

....

....

Date: day .... month .... year ....
The weather was:
sunny ☐ cloudy ☐ rainy ☐ snowy ☐

07 Fly a kite

Not every day is the perfect day for kite flying but it's always fun to try.

What you need:
- Plenty of wind
- A wide open space
- A kite!

Top tip for success:
For your kite to really fly, it needs a nice clear sky and a large open space – look up and check nothing will get in the way.

It's not that hard to make your own kite – all you need is a big piece of plastic, lots of string, some tape, 2 bamboo BBQ skewers and a bit of help. Give it a go!

A kite needs an average wind to be able to fly, usually between four and ten miles an hour. If the leaves on the trees are hardly moving, there may be too little wind to fly the kite, but if they're rustling and flags are waving, there is usually enough wind. However, if the trees are bending over in the wind, it's probably too strong.

Launching

- With your back to the wind, hold the kite as high as you can with its nose facing upwards. Don't throw it – let the wind take it.
- As the kite starts to rise, let the flying line out a little – it will dip but that's OK. Before it gets too low, tighten the line and the kite will rise again.
- Keep doing this until the kite rises up into steady winds.
- If the wind is very light, get a friend to hold the kite about 15 metres away. Both of you stand in a straight line with the wind, then release the kite. As you pull on the line, it will rise.

Take care!

Keep away from power lines, cars and roads, and don't fly your kite with people right below it.

Date: day .... month .... year ....

The weather was:

sunny ☐ cloudy ☐ rainy ☐ snowy ☐

08 Catch a fish with a net

Fast swimmers and slippery when wet, you have to be quick to catch a fish!

What you need:
- Somewhere fish live (the sea, a river, a canal or a lake)
- Somewhere you can stand or sit for a while safely
- A net
- Get permission from the person that owns the land

Top tip for success:
Fishing takes time and patience: find someone who knows all about fishing to help you catch a whopper. Fish like where they live and want to stay there. Always put them quickly back in the water. For more help and advice on fishing, visit www.nationaltrust.org.uk/50things

What fish did you catch?
Draw a picture here and give it a name!

Size of fish: ....

Type of fish: ....

Name of fish: ....

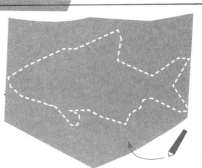

In seawater, try to net:
- The Fifteen-spined Stickleback is brown or olive green and it can grow up to a whopping 19cm. You may find it in rock pools and shallow water.
- Goby – different types of this small fish live in sandy shallows, rock pools and estuaries. They have blunt heads, two dorsal fins and big eyes and lips.
- Shrimp have five pairs of legs, grow up to 9cm long and are found on muddy and sandy shores. They change colour to match their surroundings.
- Prawns live in rock pools. They are greyish brown, have four pairs of legs and grow up to 11cm.

In freshwater, try to net:
- Minnows are small olive-green fish, which can grow as big as 8-10cm.
- The Three-spined Stickleback is silvery-blue or green and measures just 6-10cm. It has three distinct spines on its back.

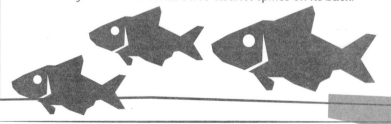

Date: day .... month .... year ....
The weather was:
sunny ☐ cloudy ☐ rainy ☐ snowy ☐

09 Eat an apple straight from a tree

Money may not grow on trees but apples do!

What you need:
- An apple tree – with eating apples
- Somebody to help you reach the branches

Top tip for success:
The ripest apples are on the outside branches,
furthest away from the trunk. Don't eat raw cooking apples –
they could give you a tummy ache!

What will you do with all your apples? You could make an apple
crumble – it's really yummy and easy to make with a grown-up to
help you with the sharp bits and the hot bits.

Ingredients:

For the crumble topping:
300g plain flour
pinch of salt
175g brown sugar
200g unsalted butter

For the filling:
450g eating apples –
peeled, cored and
cut into 1cm cubes
25g brown sugar
1 tbsp plain flour

Instructions:
1. Turn the oven on to 180 degrees
2. Put the flour and sugar for the crumble
   topping in a big bowl and mix well
3. Cube the butter and rub into the flour
   and sugar with your fingers and thumbs
   until the mixture goes crumbly
4. Put all the ingredients for the filling in a
   separate bowl and mix well
5. Spoon the filling mix into an ovenproof
   dish and then spoon the crumble mix
   onto the top and bake in the oven for
   40-45 minutes

Date: day .... month .... year ....
The weather was:
sunny ☐ cloudy ☐ rainy ☐ snowy ☐

Play conkers 10

Remember, it's not always the biggest conker that wins.

What you need:
- A conker
- Some string
- A worthy opponent
- A grown-up to help you get the string through the conker

Top tip for success:
To choose a killer conker, put some conkers in a bucket of water; all those that sink to the bottom are winners, those that float are losers.

How to play conkers:
The object of the game is to smash your opponent's conker to smithereens, thereby declaring yourself the winner.

Take your trusty conker and wrap the string around your hand so that the conker hangs straight down in a calm and steady manner. There must be no tomfoolery by either player such as moving away from your opponent's conker or aiming your conker anywhere other than another conker.

Your opponent, now known to all as 'the striker', must wrap their conker string around their hand.

Using their other hand, 'the striker' will draw the conker back and release it in an attempt to thwack your conker.

Players take it in turns to repeat the steps above, until one of the conkers is smashed to smithereens.

Date: day .... month .... year ....
The weather was:
sunny ☐ cloudy ☐ rainy ☐ snowy ☐

11   Throw some snow

You don't have to be an Eskimo to
become an expert at throwing snowballs.

What you need:
- Clean snow and lots of it
- Warm, waterproof gloves

Top tip for success:
Snow that squeaks when you walk on it won't
make a great snowball because it's too dry. Listen to the
snow before you throw and go for the slightly soggier stuff.

How many snowballs would it
take to make a snowman? Ten?
One hundred? A gazillion?

Draw a snowman made
of snowballs here:

Date: day .... month .... year ....
    The weather was:
    sunny ☐ cloudy ☐ rainy ☐ snowy ☐

The beach is full of hidden treasures like shells, stones and feathers. Let us know if you find any gold.

What you need:
- A bucket
- A spade for digging

Top tip for success:
Dig around big logs and bits of driftwood – they're great hiding places for treasure.

Which of these shells did you find?

Razor Clam?

Scallop?

Oyster?

Mussel?

Date: day .... month .... year ....

The weather was:

sunny ☐ cloudy ☐ rainy ☐ snowy ☐

Recipe: Mud. More mud.

What you need:
- Lots of mud
- Stones and leaves for decorating your pie
- Optional extras include bucket, spade, water, sticks to help you move the mud around

Top tip for success:
Mud pies might look delicious but they don't taste great, so never eat a mud pie. Don't forget to wash your hands afterwards.

My muddy thumbprint:

Date: day .... month .... year ....
The weather was:
sunny ☐   cloudy ☐   rainy ☐   snowy ☐

Dam a stream

It won't be long before the stream's a pond!

What you need:
- Twigs
- Branches
- Stones
- Rocks

Top tip for success:
What goes up must come down – have fun smashing down the dam once you've made it but don't go in too deep.

Time taken to build the dam:

....

Time taken for the dam to burst:

....

Date: day .... month .... year ....
The weather was:
sunny ☐ cloudy ☐ rainy ☐ snowy ☐

15 Go sledging

Remember sledges don't have brakes! Don't forget to scream!

What you need:
- A sledge
- Plenty of snow
- A hill that's not too steep for sledging
- Plenty of space at the bottom and nothing you might bump into
- Winter woollies

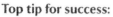

Top tip for success:
Always go feet first, so if you're going too fast you can plunge your feet into the snow and brake!

Time taken to get to the bottom of the hill:

Run 1 ....

Run 2 ....

Run 3 ....

Run 4 ....

Date: day .... month .... year ....

The weather was:

sunny ☐ cloudy ☐ rainy ☐ snowy ☐

Don't forget to leave their head sticking out so they can smile for the camera!

What you need:
- A sandy beach
- Somebody who's willing to get buried
- A spade

Top tip for success:
If the person being buried won't keep still, tell them the more they wiggle, the longer it will take.

Stick your photo here:

Date: day .... month .... year ....

The weather was:

sunny ☐ cloudy ☐ rainy ☐ snowy ☐

17 Set up a snail race

On your marks, get set, go…slowly!

What you need:
- Some snails
- A circle of chalk to mark your finish line
- Team colours for your snails (stickers work well)

Top tip for success:
Snails are slow movers. Try speeding your snail up by tempting it towards the finish line with some tasty looking leaves. Put the snails back where they came from after the race – imagine how long it would take them to get home!

Keep a record of the winner:

Race number	Winning snail	Trained by

Date: day .... month .... year ....
The weather was:
sunny ☐ cloudy ☐ rainy ☐ snowy ☐

You'd have to be mad to balance on a tree that was still standing.

What you need:
- A large tree that's lying on the ground
- Trainers or boots – leave your flip-flops behind

Top tip for success:
Check the tree is not too slippery before you start. Balancing is easier when you put your arms out to the side.

What made the tree fall to the ground? Write your ideas here:

....

....

....

Date: day .... month .... year ....

The weather was:

sunny ☐ cloudy ☐ rainy ☐ snowy ☐

19 Swing on a rope swing

Make like Tarzan and swing from a rope. Hold on tight!

What you need:
· A ready-made rope swing securely fixed onto a sturdy branch (get a grown-up to check it before you swing)

Top tip for success:
It may feel weird at first but for maximum swing, hold on to the rope and jump backwards to get started. Don't hold the rope too high up. Please visit www.nationaltrust.org.uk/50things for information from the Forestry Commission on how to rope swing safely.

What would be the worst thing to swing over?

1. A pit of poisonous snakes .... ☐

2. Shark-infested water .... ☐

3. A gang of hungry crocodiles .... ☐

4. A pond of green slime .... ☐

- You need to be quite big and strong to have fun on a rope swing.
- Before using the swing, check all the knots are firm, then sit on it without swinging to make sure it will take your weight. Get someone bigger and heavier to test it, too!
- When you climb on, cross your legs tightly to help stop you slipping off.
- Hold on to the rope tightly with both hands.
- Once you have tried out the swing, close your eyes and feel the wind rushing past as you fly through the air.
- Don't go on a rope wearing flip-flops – they might fly off!

Date: day .... month .... year ....
The weather was:
sunny ☐ cloudy ☐ rainy ☐ snowy ☐

20 Make a mud slide

It's slippery and messy so mud makes the perfect slide.

What you need:
- A muddy hill
- A bin liner (optional)
- Make sure there is plenty of space at the bottom and nothing you might bump into

Top tip for success:
The more times you slide, the slipperier it gets. You can use the bin liner to sit on and slide or to stick your muddy clothes in afterwards!

I got mud on my...

Bottom ☐

Hands ☐

Nose ☐

Hair ☐

Shoes ☐

Ears ☐

Date: day .... month .... year ....

The weather was:

sunny ☐ cloudy ☐ rainy ☐ snowy ☐

Find your own food and take it home in your tummy.

What you need:
- Bushes full of blackberries
- Help from a grown-up who knows what they're doing

Top tip for success:
September is a prime time to pick blackberries from hedgerows – they're everywhere!
We've lots of help online at
www.nationaltrust.org.uk/50things

Can you draw a blackberry with your fingers just using blackberry juice?

Date: day .... month .... year ....
The weather was:
sunny ☐ cloudy ☐ rainy ☐ snowy ☐

22 Take a look inside a tree

Some trees have hollows so big you can climb right inside.

What you need:
· A tree with a big hole in it

Top tip for success:
The oldest trees have the biggest hollows
so look for the big tall trees.

Legend has it, Robin Hood and his merry men used to shelter in a
hollow oak tree and often stored their treasure there. What kind of
things would they keep in the tree?

....

....

....

....

....

Date: day .... month .... year ....

The weather was:

sunny ☐ cloudy ☐ rainy ☐ snowy ☐

Some islands are so tiny you can walk from one end to the other.

What you need:
- An island
- Transport to and from the island

Top tip for success:
Find out how big the island is and how long it would take to walk from one end to the other. You might be surprised!

How did you get to the island?

I swam ☐

I walked ☐

I went on a causeway ☐

I rode a dolphin ☐

I went on a ferry ☐

I went on a pirate ship ☐

Date: day .... month .... year ....
The weather was:
sunny ☐ cloudy ☐ rainy ☐ snowy ☐

24 Feel like you're flying in the wind

Lean into the wind and spread your wings (or arms, if you're a human).

What you need:
- A really windy day
- A wide open space

Top tip for success:
For maximum effect, go to the top of a hill but stay away from steep edges (because you're not actually a bird, remember).

If you could be any bird, which bird would you be and why?

☐ An eagle

☐ A robin

☐ A swallow

☐ A pigeon

☐ A seagull

Date: day .... month .... year ....

The weather was:

sunny ☐ cloudy ☐ rainy ☐ snowy ☐

Blow into a blade of grass and start up the band.

What you need:
- A clean, wide blade of grass
- A big breath
- 2 hands

Top tip for success:
For the loudest squeak, make a hole in the grass with your fingernail then position the grass right in between your thumbs and press your lips firmly together before you blow.

Stick your grass trumpet here.

Date: day .... month .... year ....
The weather was:

sunny ☐   cloudy ☐   rainy ☐   snowy ☐

26   Hunt for fossils and bones

There aren't many dinosaur bones around these days but you never know what other treasure you might find if you dig around.

What you need:
· Bucket and spade

Top tip for success:
Dogs are known for burying their bones and anything else they can lay their paws on. When you're digging around, make sure you're not digging up what some dog has left behind.

Make sure you know
The Fossil Code:

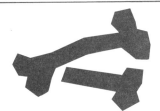

1. Stay away from cliffs
2. Don't hammer or dig in cliffs
3. Keep away from cliff edges
4. Always go collecting when the tide is going out
5. Be aware of weather conditions
6. You can collect things which have been naturally unearthed or washed up, but don't dig up stuff where it was originally buried
7. Make sure you take a grown-up with you

Record keeping
Always make a note of exactly where and when you found your fossil and label it when you get it home.

Examine pebbles and rocks on the beach for evidence of prehistoric life. Fossils occur when a dead creature is preserved in rock.

You may not find a dinosaur, but all sorts of interesting beasties are fossilized. Most are found in sedimentary rocks, which are formed when sediment – sand, clay, silt and bits of shell – builds up on the seafloor, or in rivers and lakes. Geological maps show the best areas to hunt for fossils – the coast and quarries are good locations.

Timing
- The best time to hunt on the coast is just after a storm when the waves may have uncovered new finds, so fossil hunting is a brilliant activity in winter and spring.
- To be safe, start hunting just as the tide is going out – check with the local coastguard for details of the tides.
- Never chisel away at cliffs. Eyes are best – plenty of fossils can be found without hammers and chisels.
- Go on an organised fossil hunt with an expert.

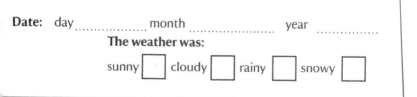

Date: day .... month .... year ....
The weather was:
sunny ☐ cloudy ☐ rainy ☐ snowy ☐

And listen to its very own bird alarm clock.

What you need:
- An alarm clock or someone to wake you up early
- A torch
- A warm coat

Top tip for success:
It may sound mad but you will need to wake up in the dark or you'll be too late.

How many birds could you hear singing?
Which colours could you see in the sky?......................................

....

....

....

....

Date: day .... month .... year ....
The weather was:
sunny ☐ cloudy ☐ rainy ☐ snowy ☐

Climb a huge hill 28

Get to the top and touch the sky.

What you need:
- A huge hill
- A footpath to take you to the top
- Trainers or boots – leave your flip-flops behind

Top tip for success:
It might take a while to get up but it doesn't take so long to get down. If the hill is really huge, walking up might seem like hard work at times. But don't forget there's nothing better than a sing-song to keep spirits up. Stay away from drops and edges.

Stick in your photo of the view from the top or draw what you saw:

Date: day .... month .... year ....

The weather was:

sunny ☐ cloudy ☐ rainy ☐ snowy ☐

29 Get behind a waterfall

Who knew water could be so noisy?

What you need:
- A waterfall
- If you want to stay dry, you might want to take a towel or a raincoat
- Trainers or boots – leave your flip-flops behind
- A grown-up to help you

Top tip for success:
The rocks around the waterfall will be slippery – crawl on hands and knees if you need to.

Find out where the waterfall came from or if it has a name: ....

....

....

....

....

Date: day .... month .... year ....

The weather was:

sunny ☐ cloudy ☐ rainy ☐ snowy ☐

Shape your hand like a plate and don't worry about the cutlery – beaks provided!

What you need:
- Some birdseed or breadcrumbs
- A hand

Top tip for success:
Don't flap about or they won't stick around, and wash your hands afterwards – those beaks get seriously sticky!

I fed: [choose a name]

who is a: [type of bird]

Write 3 things about this type of bird:

1

2

3

Date: day .... month .... year ....
The weather was:
sunny ☐ cloudy ☐ rainy ☐ snowy ☐

31 Hunt for bugs

What's the creepiest crawly you can find?

What you need:
- Places where bugs like to hide –
  under rocks, in the mud, in the
  bark of fallen trees

Top tip for success:
Remember you're a giant compared to these little beasts so be gentle - take a look before you touch. You might be having too much fun to want to go home but bugs like where they live so make sure you put them back.

Draw the best bug you found:

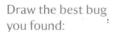

Insects outnumber humans by 250,000 to one, and in the UK there are more than 21,000 different kinds.
- A magnified container is a brilliant way to study a bug.
- Put an old towel or sheet (ask permission first) under a bush and shake the twigs and branches – you'll be amazed at how many bugs fall onto the cloth.
- Dampen some old newspapers with water. Leave them in the garden for several days before checking what's come to live underneath them.

Beetles

Everybody can recognise a ladybird but there are many more types of beetle. Like butterflies, they have different life-cycle stages – eggs, larvae and pupae – and can be as beautiful as butterflies.

Ants

Ants are great bugs to hunt – they can be found everywhere and there are 50 different varieties in the UK. The black garden ant is the most common. Watch them to see what they eat and try to spot them working as teams, carrying large insects or pieces of twigs back to their nest.

Date: day .... month .... year ....
The weather was:
sunny ☐ cloudy ☐ rainy ☐ snowy ☐

32 Find some frogspawn

You think frogspawn looks weird? Just wait until they become tadpoles!

What you need:
- A bucket or a plastic tub
- A net can be helpful to scoop them out
- A grown-up to supervise while you scoop
- Somewhere you can stand or sit for a while safely

Top tip for success:
Don't take the frogspawn away – they're happy in their home. Once you've had a look, put them back in the pond.

Draw what you saw:

What shape is the black dot in the jelly? Can you see a tail? Or even legs?

- The female frog does not lay eggs until she is five years old. She lays 3,000 plus eggs in one go in February or March, but only five of her babies are likely to grow into frogs.
- Frogspawn is the name for the clusters of eggs.
- The eggs sink to the bottom of the water and are protected by a thick coating of jelly.
- Over time this jelly starts to swell and the eggs float to the surface, where they're warmed by the sun.

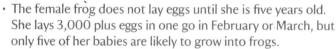

- The baby frogs – tadpoles – hatch out after a few weeks. To begin with, they eat the jelly that surrounded them, but after a few days they start eating pondweed.
- Tadpoles usually turn into frogs in July. The whole process – from egg to tadpole to young frog – takes about 12 weeks.

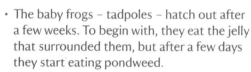

Date: day .... month .... year ....

The weather was:

sunny ☐ cloudy ☐ rainy ☐ snowy ☐

33 Catch a butterfly in a net

They won't mind if you say hello, just so long as you let them go.

What you need:
- A butterfly net
  (or a shrimping net will do)

Top tip for success:
Nobody wants to squash a butterfly, so catch them with care – stop the net stroke as soon as the butterfly is in the net, and flip the net over to prevent the butterfly escaping.
Some butterflies are very rare so we're not allowed to catch them.
Visit www.nationaltrust.org.uk/50things to find out more.

What type of butterfly
did you see?
Draw what you saw:

Catching a butterfly is stupendous, but seeing it fly away is even better. Butterflies damage easily, so always place your net very gently over a settled butterfly (a shrimping net is OK). Put the butterfly in a clear plastic box to look at it, but if it beats its wings hard pop the box into a dark place for a few minutes first. Let the butterfly go as soon as possible in the same place you found it, especially if it's getting unhappy.

It's against the law to catch some types of butterfly (log on to www.butterfly-conservation.org), and you shouldn't catch them on a nature reserve unless you're with the warden or ranger. If possible, go on a butterfly-spotting walk with an expert who can teach you all about butterflies and where they live.

Record keeping
The best way to remember the butterflies you've seen is to photograph them. Then you can study the colours and patterns on their wings and do drawings of them.

Date: day................. month .... year ....
The weather was:
sunny ☐ cloudy ☐ rainy ☐ snowy ☐

34 Track wild animals

Animals are easy to find if you follow their footprints, feathers, fur and poo.

What you need:
- Sharp eyes
- Trainers or boots – leave your flip-flops behind

Top tip for success:
Remember, animals don't wear shoes so their footprints don't all look the same. From a horse's hoof to a rabbit's paw, learn what you're looking for. Whatever you do, don't touch the poo!

What I tracked:

	Tick
Hoof prints	
Feathers	
Fur	
Paw prints	
Bird prints	
Poo	

Track wild animals when the ground is soft and wet or, even better, in the snow. In some species, the front and rear paw prints are slightly different. To help identify them, go to: www.bbc.co.uk/nature/animals/wildbritain/field_guides/animal_tracks. Look out for the following:

- Badgers stick to regular pathways, so once you've found a track, you'll find another one. The badger has five toes and a kidney-shaped pad.
- Foxes wander all over the place and their paw prints are similar to a dog's. They have four toes – the front two are close together – and a rear pad.
- Deer have cloven hooves, so only two toes.
- Rats and squirrels have four long toes and claws; their tracks look a bit like a handprint.
- Rabbits have four toes – their tracks are easy to spot because of their long hind legs.

Date: day .... month .... year ....

The weather was:

sunny ☐ cloudy ☐ rainy ☐ snowy ☐

35 Discover what's in a pond

Murky pond water is full of life. Scoop some out into a tub and check out what lurks beneath.

What you need:
- A clean, empty plastic tub
- A fine net
- Somewhere you can stand or sit for a while safely

Top tip for success:
Scoop the net 3 times in a figure of 8 to pick up the most tiny creatures and empty the contents into the tub. If you don't spot anything at first, take a closer look. Pond life tends to be quite tiny. Return the mini-beasts to their homes.

Draw what you saw:

All sorts of creatures can be found in ponds as well as fish and tadpoles: small mammals, such as water shrews and rats, and watery creepy-crawlies like water snails and water spiders. Ponds are also full of developing youngsters: frogs, newts, dragonflies and damselflies all lay their eggs in the water. Mosquitoes love water and their eggs provide food for fish and larvae.

- Newts are easiest to see in spring when they return to ponds to breed.
- Water boatmen are insects that rest on the surface. They use their back legs like oars to move through the water and dive down to catch tadpoles and insect larvae. They can nip, so take care.
- The Great Diving Beetle grows to about 5cm long and is black with yellow around the edge of its wings. It eats small fish and tadpoles and dives deep into the water in search of food. It will bite you if you handle it.

Date: day .... month .... year ....
The weather was:
sunny ☐ cloudy ☐ rainy ☐ snowy ☐

36 Call an owl

Owls might not have mobiles but if you call an owl, it will call you right back.

What you need:
- An excellent owl impression
- A torch
- Something to sit on

Top tip for success:
Most owls come out at night so wait until it's dark to catch them at their chattiest. An expert guide will help you get the most out of the experience and keep you safe. Visit www.nationaltrust.org.uk/50things to find out more.

What would you like to ask an owl?
If you were a wizard, what kind of owl would you choose?

....

....

....

....

Date: day .... month .... year ....

The weather was:

sunny ☐ cloudy ☐ rainy ☐ snowy ☐

What's the weirdest looking thing you can find?

What you need:
- A clean plastic tub or bucket to scoop the water out
- A small net to help you catch things
- A low tide

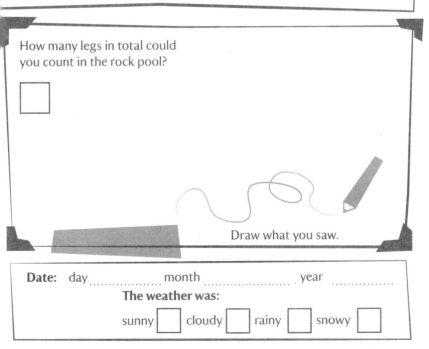

Top tip for success:
Keep your hands out of the pool or you might feel a little nibble or pinch! These crazy creatures like where they live – put them back in the pool when you've taken a look.

How many legs in total could you count in the rock pool?

Draw what you saw.

Date: day .... month .... year ....
The weather was:
sunny ☐ cloudy ☐ rainy ☐ snowy ☐

38   Bring up a butterfly

Once a caterpillar makes its cocoon, it may become a
beautiful butterfly in less than two weeks.

What you need:
- Caterpillar
- Large plastic tub with small holes in the lid
- Leaves from one of the caterpillar's
  favourite plants
- Slightly damp soil or sand to line the
  bottom of the tub
- A twig or two to lean against the side of the tub

Top tip for success:
Avoid hairy caterpillars as some can sting. Visit
www.nationaltrust.org.uk/50things for more advice
on how to choose and look after your caterpillar.

Caterpillar diary

Date I put the caterpillar in the tub: ....

Date the caterpillar made a cocoon: ....

Date I set the butterfly free: ....

Colour of caterpillar: ....

Colour of cocoon: ....

Colour of butterfly: ....

- If you don't want to take a caterpillar from the wild, order a farmed one through the post.
- It's difficult to feed and care for loads of caterpillars, so only keep a few.
- Some caterpillars can be kept in clean, clear plastic boxes – add some plant food every day.
- Keep the boxes clean – remove droppings and condensation daily.
- Caterpillars must be kept out of hot sun or they will bake in a small box. A window that gets early morning sun is best.

- Red Admiral, Orange Tip and Comma caterpillars are best reared on the cut stems of their plant food standing in a vase. Put cotton wool around the top of the vase to stop the caterpillars crawling in.
- Don't handle caterpillars that aren't crawling around – they might be changing their skins or pupating.
- Allow your butterflies' wings to harden off properly before releasing them where their plant food grows.

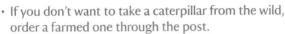

Date: day .... month .... year ....
The weather was:
sunny ☐ cloudy ☐ rainy ☐ snowy ☐

39 Catch a crab

With the right bait and a piece of string it's easier than you might think.

What you need:
- String or crab line
- A good spot by the sea to get settled
- Scraps of bacon or fish for the bait
- A bucket of water if you'd like to take a closer look before they go back in

Top tip for success:
Tie the stone to the end of the string so it sinks properly. When you feel it tugging, pull the string up at a good pace – too fast and the crab will fall off, too slowly and it will eat all the bait! Be very careful when you pick them up (they're not afraid to use those pincers) and then put them back in the water.

How long did it take you to catch your first crab?

☐ 1 minute (I guess I got lucky)

☐ 5 minutes (I'm a crabbing genius)

☐ 1 hour (I'm not bad at this crabbing business!)

☐ 3 days (I am very patient and determined)

There are 50 types of crab in the UK – some are found only far out at sea but others live in shallow water or rock pools. They often bury themselves in wet sand or mud or hide under seaweed. Crabs have a thick skeleton and a single pair of claws, and they typically walk sideways. Male crabs often have bigger claws than females.

Picking up a crab
Crabbing is great fun but you must be careful or you could hurt or even kill the crabs. You can pick up a crab with your fingers from a rock pool, but be careful as they can pinch. You may need a crabbing line to catch them in slightly deeper water.

Catching a crab
- Have a net handy to pop under the crab to prevent it falling back into the water.
- Keep crabs in seawater in a bucket but don't leave it in direct sunshine.
- Crabs get very unhappy and may fight if they are kept together, so don't keep more than a few in a bucket at any one time.
- Always put your crabs back in the water where you found them.

Date: day .... month .... year ....
The weather was:
sunny ☐ cloudy ☐ rainy ☐ snowy ☐

40 Go on a nature walk at night

Some creatures only come out at night so this is the only chance you've got of spotting them!

What you need:
- A torch
- A grown-up who can show you where to look
- Trainers or boots – leave the slippers at home
- Warm clothing (pyjamas don't count)

Top tip for success:
Only use your torch when you really need to.
These animals aren't afraid of the dark! They are afraid of noisy humans though so be as quiet as a mouse.

Draw what you saw:

Lots of creatures are nocturnal – most active at night – so if you want to see owls, bats, hedgehogs, foxes, badgers and otters, as well as masses of moths, you'll need to venture out in the dark. Go with an adult or join an organised walk with an expert.

- You don't have to wait until the middle of the night – nocturnal animals get busy as soon as it gets dark.
- Stay very quiet – animals have good hearing and if you make lots of noise or your clothes rustle they will sense danger and go into hiding.
- Keep your ears open – you will hear bats and owls before you see them.
- Look out for tracks, droppings and signs of feeding – deer make a terrible mess.
- Take a lamp outside, shine it onto an old white sheet and wait for the moths to arrive – you will be able to see them clearly.

Date: day .... month .... year ....

The weather was:

sunny ☐ cloudy ☐ rainy ☐ snowy ☐

41 Plant it, grow it, eat it

Just like you, fruit and vegetables need a bit of time to grow but they're definitely worth the wait.

What you need:
- Fruit or vegetable plant or seeds
- Pot to plant them in
- Peat-free compost

Top tip for success:
Make sure you plant the right thing at the right time. Visit www.eatseasonably.co.uk for all the info you need to grow your own.

Planting diary

Date planted:

....

I first spotted fruit/veg on: [date]

....

I first ate something from my plant on: [date]

....

Nothing tastes as delicious as food you've grown yourself and it's so easy to do. Plant your absolute favourite things to eat (see also pages 102–107).

- Fruit trees produce lots of fruit but you must wait a few years.
- Soft fruit, such as raspberries and strawberries, will give you a crop quite quickly, but you'll need more than one plant to give your family plenty to eat.

- Vegetables grow much faster than fruit.
- Tomatoes are easy to grow – decide if you want tiny cherry toms or great, fat, round beef tomatoes.
- Courgettes grow so fast they become giant marrows if you turn your back on them for a moment.
- Pumpkins are the heaviest things to grow – they can become ENORMOUS.
- Peas and beans shoot up really quickly.

- Sow salad greens a few seeds at a time, and then sow a few more every week to get a steady supply through the summer.
- Everybody loves potatoes – dig them up and cook them as and when you need them.

Date: day .... month .... year ....
The weather was:
sunny ☐ cloudy ☐ rainy ☐ snowy ☐

42 Go wild swimming

Lake, river or sea: it's much more fun than swimming in a pool.

What you need:
- Lake, river or sea
- Advice from an expert on the best spot for swimming safely
- Goggles
- Take a grown-up with you

Top tip for success:
The best thing about wild swimming is the view (and the fact you won't catch a verruca!).

My swimming diary

I swam in: river / lake / sea

I wore: swimming costume / wetsuit / snorkel and flippers

The water was: freezing / chilly / quite nice actually / as warm as a bath

I stayed in for: [   ] minutes

Wild swimming is one of the most exciting and fun things you can do. Surf the waves in the sea and feel the sand and salt on your skin. Streams, ponds, rivers and lakes are just as great and the water isn't salty. Let the gentle current carry you along a stream or feel the fish nibbling your toes in a pond – lie on your back, float and look at the sky above. It will be a magic moment you will remember forever.

Safety is important
- Always make sure an adult knows exactly where you are and what you're doing.
- If you're on the beach, look for flags to tell you whether or not it's safe to swim.
- Rivers can have fast and dangerous currents, just like the sea.
- Don't get too cold – if your teeth are chattering, it's time to come out and warm up.
- Don't swim in dirty water or in forests of weed as your legs can get tangled in it.
- Be aware that the depth of the water can change very suddenly.

Date: day .... month .... year ....
The weather was:
sunny ☐ cloudy ☐ rainy ☐ snowy ☐

43 Go rafting

Not your average way to get from A to B.

What you need:
- A raft
- A river or lake
- A lifejacket
- Paddles
- Some help from an expert

Top tip for success:
Paddle hard and don't stand up! This isn't the kind of thing you do everyday – join a class or go to an event.
Visit www.nationaltrust.org.uk/50things to find out more.

Photo of me
on a raft:

Nothing is more fun than building your own raft – big or small – and trying to sail it, although spills are likely! Rafts can be made from thin wooden logs bound together, pieces of driftwood and even plastic water bottles. If you're building a tiny raft, use corks and lollipop sticks, or just twigs and string. The basic principle is the same whatever size you're making.

Build your own raft
- Make the rectangular deck by tying branches together or use one big, flat piece of wood.
- Put two or three pieces of wood at right angles to the base and tie them together very tightly. Alternatively, collect masses of empty screw-top plastic bottles to create buoyancy, place them on top of a net, put the base on top, pull the net taut and secure this to the top of the raft.
- Make paddles and even a sail.
- Only ever launch a raft with adult supervision.

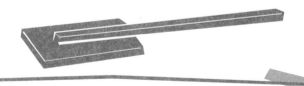

Date: day .... month .... year ....
The weather was:
sunny ☐ cloudy ☐ rainy ☐ snowy ☐

44 Light a fire without matches

Serious survival skills required.

What you need:
- A clear, dry spot to build a fire
- Dry tinder (dry grass, bracken or moss; cotton wool also works nicely but it doesn't grow in the wild so you'll need to supply your own)
- Some expert help

Top tip for success:
This is without a doubt one of the trickiest things in the book. Find someone who knows what they're doing for the best chance of success.

How did you light your fire without matches?

....

....

....

....

How long did it take you to get the fire going? ....

Get everything ready before you start

As well as dry tinder (see opposite), you will need:
- Dry kindling – small to medium twigs
- Dry fuel – larger branches and logs.

Making a spark
- **Solar energy** – if it's sunny, you can use a magnifying glass to ignite the tinder. Hold the lens about 30cm from the tinder nest and keep the focus on one spot. When the tinder starts to smoulder, blow on it to ignite the flames, then put some kindling on top.
- **Fire by friction** – find a straight stick and a flat piece of dry wood or bark with a groove in it. Put the point of the stick in the groove and rub the stick very quickly between your hands. The wood will heat until it creates a small ember, which can be dropped into the tinder nest. This is easier if you loop a piece of string or a shoelace around the stick and move the string back and forth to make the stick spin faster.

Safety tips
- Keep your wood supply well away from the fire.
- Never leave a fire unattended.
- Don't make your fire close to flammable materials.
- Make sure you put out the fire (with water if necessary) before leaving.
- Always make sure an adult is there to supervise you.
- Have a supply of water handy, in case you need to put out the fire or soothe burns.

Date: day .... month .... year ....
The weather was:
  sunny ☐ cloudy ☐ rainy ☐ snowy ☐

You'll never get lost if you can use these trusty tools.

What you need:

- A map
- A compass
- A destination
- A whistle to let people know where you are

Top tip for success:

Always work out where you are on the map before you even set off so you know you're starting in the right place. It also helps if you hold the map the right way round!

Draw your own map of where you went:

Date: day .... month .... year ....

The weather was:

sunny ☐ cloudy ☐ rainy ☐ snowy ☐

Try bouldering 46

Sounds crazy but it's rock climbing without the ropes!

What you need:
- The right kind of rocks
- The right kind of clothes (nothing that will get in the way)
- The right kind of trainers or boots – definitely leave your flip-flops behind!
- Expert advice and supervision

Top tip for success:
Not the kind of thing you do everyday – join a class or go to an event. Visit www.nationaltrust.org.uk/50things to find out more. Build up slowly and soon you'll be bouldering Bond-style.

Stick a photo of you bouldering here:

Date: day .... month .... year ....

The weather was:

sunny ☐ cloudy ☐ rainy ☐ snowy ☐

47 Cook on a campfire

There's no kitchen in the great outdoors but you don't have to miss dinner!

What you need:
- Campfire
- Your chosen ingredients
- Cooking equipment such as skewers for your marshmallows, a pot for your beans or a pan for your bangers
- A grown-up to check you don't spoil dinner

Top tip for success:
This is not the time for a Sunday roast with all the trimmings. Keep it simple at first with food that cooks quickly and easily. Sausages, soups or beans all work well.

My campfire menu

My starter: ....

My main course: ....

My dessert: ....

- Some foods are really easy to cook on a fire. All you need to do is wrap them up in kitchen foil, then pop them into the fire to cook – perfect for baked potatoes, which take about an hour, and corn on the cob, which cooks in about 15 minutes.
- Fillets of fish or chicken are quick and easy cooked in foil, too – pop some vegetables in with them.
- Bananas only take 10 minutes, in their skin and wrapped in foil, or peel them and put some chunks of chocolate inside the skin before wrapping them up tightly again – hot bananas with chocolate sauce are delicious!
- Cook things on a stick – hot dogs are easy to warm up, and toasted marshmallows are yummy.
- Cook in a frying pan – nothing beats a fantastic fry-up of sausages, bacon, tomatoes, mushrooms and eggs, but don't turn your back on the pan.

Date: day .... month .... year ....
The weather was:
sunny ☐ cloudy ☐ rainy ☐ snowy ☐

48 Try abseiling

The daring adventure that you really shouldn't miss.

What you need:
- This is one adventure that requires some serious equipment. It's highly unlikely you will have this kind of stuff lying around at home

Top tip for success:
Not the kind of thing you do everyday –
join a class or go to an event.
Visit www.nationaltrust.org.uk/50things to find out more.

Stick a photo of you
abseiling here:

Date: day .... month .... year ....
The weather was:
sunny ☐ cloudy ☐ rainy ☐ snowy ☐

With over a million in the world, there must be one around here somewhere…

What you need:
· A smartphone or a handheld GPS

Top tip for success:
Get involved and join a geocache community online. The largest is www.geocaching.com

Find a geocache

Hunting for a geocache is like combining hide and seek with a treasure hunt. A cache is a small container with a logbook in which you enter the date you found it. It sometimes contains small trinkets that can be exchanged. The co-ordinates are put on a listing site; geocaches may be easy or hard to find, and while some are big, others are tiny. Give it a try and see what you find.

Place I found my geocache: ....

Where my geocache was hidden: ....

What was inside my geocache: ....

Date: day .... month .... year ....
The weather was:
sunny ☐ cloudy ☐ rainy ☐ snowy ☐

50 Canoe down a river

See the world from a duck's point of view.

What you need:
- A canoe
- Paddles
- A lifejacket
- A river
- Expert advice and supervision

Top tip for success:
Going round and round in circles can get a bit boring. Paddle evenly on both sides to go in a straight line and actually get somewhere. This isn't the kind of thing you do everyday
– join a class or go to an event.
Visit www.nationaltrust.org.uk/50things to find out more.

Name of river:...

When I was canoeing I saw:...

....

....

If you paddle the correct way, canoeing becomes much easier:

- Sit up straight and put your top hand over the top of the paddle.
- Put the other hand on the throat of the paddle – this arm creates the power of the stroke.
- Hold the paddle up out of the water and point the blade to the front of the canoe.
- Put the blade of the paddle into the water at right angles.
- Pull the paddle back in a straight line – this powers the canoe forward.
- When the blade has moved past your body in the water, lift it out and start again.

Paddling a canoe with two of you in it is harder than it looks. The person in the stern (rear) of the canoe controls the direction you go in. The bow (front) and stern paddlers should always paddle on opposite sides of the canoe.

Date: day .... month .... year ....
The weather was:

sunny ☐ cloudy ☐ rainy ☐ snowy ☐

50
MORE IDEAS
OF
FUN THINGS
TO DO
OUTDOORS

At the Seaside

In the Rain

In the Winter

In the Spring

In the Garden

At the Seaside

Hunt for hag stones

Hag stones, which are also called Witch Stones and Fairy Stones, have naturally formed holes running through them.

- It takes running water hundreds of years to make these tiny, smooth holes.
- People used to believe that hag stones protected them from bad luck and hung them up outside their houses to bring them good luck.
- The stones are said to bring good luck only if you find them yourself, or are given them by someone who loves you.
- On some beaches you'll find lots of hag stones, while, on others, you'll have to hunt very hard.
- Tie a few hag stones on a length of string, then hang them up at home to remind you of the seaside.

Chase the waves

Chase the waves on the shore line as they slip back into the sea, then run away from the next breaking wave to stop it catching you. The splashes will get you quite wet!

Collect seashells

See how many different types of seashell you can find and try to discover what type of creature the empty ones belonged to.

Explore a cave

Caves occur when the sea wears away rock in one place. They can be very deep and long and go underground for miles, or they can be quite tiny. Caves are fun to explore but do take care and check the tides before you explore.

- Always tell a grown-up that you want to look inside a cave.
- Wear sensible shoes and warm clothes – caves are cold and can be slippery.
- Take a torch if you have one, so you can look at the rocks inside the cave.
- Never go into a cave if rocks are falling nearby.

Track a set of footprints

Footprints show up clearly on sandy beaches, especially when the sand is wet. Pick an interesting footprint and try to follow it for a little while to see where it goes and who it belongs to.

Make a shell garden

- Collect tiny pebbles, shells, seaweed and interesting pieces of wood.
- Draw the edges of your garden in the sand.
- Draw in paths and flowerbeds.
- Use your finds to make paths, fences and flowerbeds.

Make a sand castle

A sand castle can be as big or as small as you like – build the kind of castle you'd like to live in, if you were a king or queen, with walls, towers and arches. Dry sand collapses easily, so it's best to use wet sand – get water from the sea in a bucket and mix it with dry sand. Pat down the sand with your hands to make a strong shape. Carve out your castle with tools: a plastic knife, a paintbrush for smoothing walls and a straw for blowing grains of sand away. A plastic spade works well for small sand castles, but if you want to build a really big one, use a garden spade.

Dig a pool and try to keep it full of seawater

Water wants to drain away through sand, but if you keep on digging deep the water will eventually start puddling at the bottom of your hole. It can be hard work, but the nearer the sea you dig the easier this will be.

Try to find four different kinds of seaweed

- There are 800 different kinds of seaweed around the British coastline.
- Seaweed comes in four colour groups: blue-greens, greens, browns and reds.
- It can grow in quite deep water as well as on the shoreline and in rock pools.
- Some kinds of seaweed are edible, but don't try to find out by tasting them.
- Dead seaweed on the shoreline changes colour and will eventually bleach white.
- Some seaweed has air pockets – or bladders – which help to lift it clear of rocks when the tide comes in.

In the Rain

Go fishing

You'll catch more fish in the rain – take a little tent and a picnic with you.

- Fish hide away on sunny days, but on cloudy days they swim about looking for food.
- Rain washes insects and bait into the water, so the fish are busy hunting for snacks.
- The rain makes it harder for the fish to see you.
- Always put any fish you have caught straight back into the water.

Play Pooh-sticks

Pooh Bear introduced the game of Pooh-sticks – you play it with a friend. All you need is a stick each and a bridge with running water below it. Throw the sticks into the water at the same time on the upstream side of the bridge, then rush to the other side – the one whose stick appears first is the winner.

Go hunting for snails – they love the rain

- There are 120 different types of snail in the UK, so there are lots to hunt.
- A snail carries its house on its back. Its shell is made mainly of chalk.
- Snails are nocturnal, but they venture out in the daytime when it's been raining.
- They can live for up to 10 years.

Jump in puddles

Put on a pair of wellington boots and a raincoat and jump in lots of puddles. Make as many big splashes as you can.

Feed the ducks

Ducks love the rain, so go out and give them some duck food – they'll be very happy to see you. Bread isn't very good for them, so offer them birdseed, oats, or defrosted frozen peas instead.

Do a chalk pavement painting

All you need is chalk, a pavement and a rainy day. It might seem funny to pick a rainy day, but chalk becomes more like paint in the wet and the colours look much brighter. Experiment with techniques and watch how the rain softens your picture.

Make a weather station/rain gauge

· Get an empty two-litre plastic water bottle.
· Cut the top off the bottle about one-quarter of the way down.
· Put the top of the bottle upside-down inside the body of the bottle – it should sit snugly.
· Place the bottle in a bucket of gravel or sand somewhere in the open – if it's close to trees or the house it won't catch the rain.
· Check it daily, using a jug to measure any rainwater collected, and record the amount.

Hunt mini-beasts under stones

If you lift up a stone you'll find that all sorts of creatures like to make their home there:

· Some centipedes, called stone dwellers, have 15 trunks, each with one pair of legs, so not all centipedes have 100 legs.
· Woodlice are related to crabs, shrimps and lobsters – they die if they get too dry.
· Although most earthworms live in deep burrows, you'll often find them under a rock.
· Earwigs like small, damp, dark places and lay their eggs under stones.

Make perfume

The wind and the rain make flowers drop their petals and no-one will mind if you pick them up – don't pull petals off flowers growing in the wild.

- Collect some petals and put them in a jar of water, then leave for a few hours before sniffing them.
- Rose petals have a lovely smell, but lots of other flowers have a wonderful perfume, too; mix them up to make your own special blend.
- The water will turn brown eventually, so it won't smell good for long.

Look for a rainbow

Look for a rainbow when the sun is shining in one part of the sky but it's raining in another part. Although sunlight looks white, it is actually made up of rainbow colours, and a rainbow occurs when the sun shines on the raindrops and breaks the light up into the different colours that are normally mixed up together. Rainbows are curved because the raindrops that reflect the sunlight are curved. You should be able to see seven colours in a rainbow, but sometimes one colour can fade.

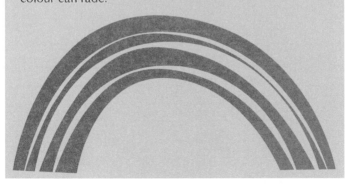

In the
Winter

Make a bird cake to feed the birds

- Make a small hole in the bottom of a yoghurt pot, thread some string through and tie a big knot on the inside.
- Cut a chunk of lard into small pieces, put it into a bowl and let it come up to room temperature.
- Add birdseed, grated cheese, raisins, and peanuts to the lard, a little at a time, and squish it all together with your fingers.
- Fill the yoghurt pot and put it in the fridge for a couple of hours to go hard before hanging it up by the string on a tree.

Collect fir cones

Fir cones contain the seeds of fir trees. They open when it's dry and close when it's wet, so they only drop their seeds in dry weather. Each type of fir tree has its own type of cone. Collect them and see how many different sorts you can find – you can make decorations out of them, too, if you paint them silver.

Make a snow angel

When it next snows, lie on your back in it and move your arms back and forth as big and wide as you can. Get up very carefully and you will see that you have left the print of an angel in the snow.

Go for a walk in the dark

Pick a night when it is frosty, wrap up warm and head out into the darkness with a grown-up. See how the frost changes the way everything looks – even pavements glitter. Leaf skeletons, seed heads and berries look magical when dusted with frost.

Look in the night sky to spot The Plough

- The patterns of stars stay the same, but they move across the sky from East to West as the earth spins.
- The Plough is one of the easiest constellations to find – seven bright stars make the shape of a saucepan with a bowl and handle.
- The bowl of the Plough points up to the North Star.

Look out for old birds' nests

- Birds nest in all sorts of places – in the cavities and branches of trees, in bushes and hedges and high up on buildings.
- They hide their nests, but old ones are sometimes uncovered when the leaves fall in autumn, or if the wind dislodges them.
- Each species of bird makes its own style of nest.
- Nests are commonly made of twigs, grass, moss, feathers, spiders' webs and mud.

Make a snowman

- To make the perfect snowman you need packing snow – snow that clumps together easily.
- Make a snowball and start to roll it along the ground – it will get bigger and bigger.
- Make three balls, the biggest goes at the bottom, the next size in the middle, and the smallest is the head at the top.
- Make a face out of anything; currants, pieces of coal, twigs, a carrot – and finish off with a hat and scarf.

93

Collect greenery, seed heads and berries

Nature has plenty of beautiful things to see in winter.
Go outside and collect dried grasses; shake seed heads
and see the seeds fly out. Look for lacy leaf skeletons
and bright berries as well as evergreen leaves, such as
ivy. Take them home and make a winter collage – use
glitter to make everything look frosty.

Build an igloo

- Make a big pile of snow, pack it down and leave it for
  half an hour – this will make it harder and stronger.
- Get an adult to help you cut bricks from this hard
  piece of snow.
- Build the igloo up by putting the bricks round and
  round in a spiral, the last block in the top needs to be
  a bit bigger than the hole.
- Pack snow into the gaps between the bricks, then dig
  a hole under one small part of the igloo and from this
  point cut out a door.

Look at frost or snow und[er a] magnifying glass

In summer we get dew in the eve[ning. In] winter when the weather is freezi[ng the dew] turns to frost. Tiny frost crystals [cover] leaves, grasses, seed heads and ev[en spiders'] webs. Take a magnifying glass outside and see how beautiful the ice crystals are. Snow crystals are even easier to see – have a close look and you'll be amazed!

In the Spring

Collect sticky buds

The big brown buds of the horse chestnut tree protect the young leaves from frost. The buds are covered with a sticky resin to keep insects out. Take them home and put them in a jar of water and watch the young leaves unfurl. When the leaf emerges, its underside is covered with fluffy white down.

Look out for birds' nests

- Birds make nests to protect themselves and their babies from cold weather.
- Nests come in all shapes and sizes.
- Birds don't only build their nests in trees and bushes – some nest on rooftops or burrows in the ground.
- Listen as well as look – baby birds call loudly for their parents when they're out getting them food.
- Don't touch the nest – you'll scare the parent birds away and their babies will starve.

Hunt for catkins

- A catkin is a cluster of small flowers that can be seen in early spring.
- All sorts of trees have catkins but especially willow, hazel and birch.
- Catkins fluff up with pollen as they blossom and this is carried off in the wind.
- Pussy willow is a catkin with fluffy silvery hairs that puff up into a yellow froth of pollen.

See newborn lambs

- Lambs are born from January onwards.
- Most sheep have one or two lambs at a time.
- Newborns are kept in special pens with their mothers.
- Lambs stand up within half an hour of their birth – with the help of their mum.
- Find out if there are lambing open days at farms in your area.

Lie under a blossom tree

Lie on your back and look up at the masses of flowers above you – far too many to count. Watch the petals come fluttering down around you like confetti.

See a spider catch a fly

The spider weaves a sticky web to catch insects. It sits in the middle, waiting for an insect to get trapped. When the insect tries to escape, the spider feels the vibrations and rushes to bite its prey with fangs that inject poison. The spider then wraps up its victim in silk to stop it damaging the web and takes it back to its den for dinner. It's fascinating stuff!

Look for ducklings

Ducks mostly stay in the water, but they make their nests on land. The female duck lays one egg a day and between eight and 18 eggs altogether. She starts sitting on the eggs when she has finished laying them all and stays with them for 28 days until they hatch. The ducklings are in their nest for less than a day before their mother leads them to the water. They feed themselves straight away but need their mum to keep them warm. They hop on her back for a ride when they're tired.

Go to see a bluebell wood
Bluebell woods in spring are very beautiful. The flowers, which appear in late April and early May, grow very, very slowly, so a bluebell wood tells you this is ancient woodland. It's tempting to pick bluebells, but please don't as they are happy where they are.

Blow a dandelion clock
The yellow dandelion is a common wild flower. As it starts to seed, the flower head turns into a mass of white parachute seeds. Blow until all the seeds are gone – the number of puffs it takes supposedly tells the hour.

Look out for the first bees of the year

- Bees die in the cold, so they can't come out to collect nectar from flowers until the temperature is high enough.
- They do an important job pollinating plants – without them we wouldn't get many seeds, berries, fruits and nuts.
- They make honey by collecting nectar from flowers.

Listen out for the cuckoo

- Cuckoos spend the winter in Africa and arrive to lay eggs in the spring.
- Only the male cuckoo calls goo-ko.
- He calls 10–20 times in a row.
- Cuckoos lay their eggs in other birds' nests.

In the Garden

Pumpkin

You can grow a pumpkin (see page 61) and eat it or carve it into a lantern for Halloween. You may need help from a grown-up for this.

- Give your pumpkin plant food every fortnight and water it if it gets dry.
- The heavy pumpkin fruit will mark if it sits on soil or grass – support it with some straw.
- Make the lid of the lantern by cutting a circle around the stalk. Next, scoop out all the soft flesh inside the pumpkin, then pop the lid back on top.
- Draw a face and cut through the skin with a knife. Make holes in the lid.

Sunflowers

Challenge a friend to see which of you can grow the tallest sunflower. The seed can be planted straight into the soil in May. Water it regularly and watch it grow tall – the flower head will follow the sun from east to west throughout the day. Keep the seeds from the flower head to feed to the birds.

Rocket

From May, plant a short line of rocket seeds every week and you and your family will have delicious, peppery salad leaves throughout the summer. These leaves are tastiest when they're young.

103

Acorns

Every mighty oak tree starts with a tiny acorn, so why not grow one yourself?

- The best time to find a good acorn is when the tree starts to drop them naturally. The acorn's ripe when it's plump and the cap comes off easily.
- Acorns need cold to germinate, so plant them in a big pot in the shade at a depth of one-and-a-half times their width and keep moist.
- Or place them in a plastic bag with some compost and put them in the fridge (not the freezer). Keep them damp until the leaves appear.
- Plant the seedling where you want it to grow as soon as the first leaves open fully.

Sweet peas

Sweet peas will give you masses of fragrant flowers that you can pick to your heart's content. The secret is to plant the seeds in September where you want them to flower. Keep your eyes open in spring and when you see the seedlings coming through make a wigwam out of bamboo canes. Wind some string around each cane in an upward spiral, so that the plants can climb. They will need masses of water. Pick the flowers – the more you pick, the more you'll get.

Avocados
The next time you eat an avocado, save the stone.

- Stick four toothpicks into the stone around the middle and balance it, pointed end upwards, on top of a glass.
- Half-cover the stone with water, and put the glass in a warm, sunny place.
- Change the water once every two days and wait for it to sprout (three to six weeks) before planting it in a pot.

Tomatoes
- Buy young tomato plants from a garden centre.
- Tomatoes need lots of warmth, so plant them in a pot or grow-bag in a sunny spot.
- Choose peat-free compost when possible – it's better for the environment.
- Water them regularly and feed them weekly with tomato feed.
- To ripen home-grown tomatoes, place them in a paper bag with a ripe tomato.

Herb garden

Plant a herb garden in the spring and learn to identify the plants by the smell of their crushed leaves. Go to a garden centre and pick some herbs you like. Plant them in a pot, or in the garden, in a sunny position. Once the plants have really started to grow, break off a few leaves and discover how nice they smell. Parsley, sage, rosemary, thyme and chives are commonly used cooking herbs that make food taste better.

Wild flowers

Turn a tiny patch of your garden into a wild flower garden and you will attract birds, butterflies and all sorts of bees. Wild flowers flourish in poor soil, so just sow the seed and wait to see what wildlife you attract.

Fruit tree

Plant a fruit tree so you can pick your favourite fruit. Most fruit trees are planted in winter and will take a few years to produce a really good crop. Watch the tree blossom in spring, then see the bees pollinating the flowers and the fruit starting to grow almost immediately. When the fruit ripens it's ready for you to pick. Learn how and when to prune the tree, so it produces lots of fruit next year, too.

50 Things events

Here's a selection of National Trust places that are holding specific 50 Things events, or which just offer the space to get mucky or try out some of the suggestions! Take a look to see which are nearest you and visit our website to find out what activities are available there. www.nationaltrust.org.uk/50things

Anglesey Abbey
Cambridgeshire

Arnside & Silverdale
Morecombe Bay, Lancashire

Ashridge Estate
Hertfordshire

Avebury
Wiltshire

Bembridge
Isle of Wight

Beningbrough Hall and Gardens
Yorkshire

Blickling Hall
Norfolk

Bodiam Castle
Sussex

Bookham & Holmwood Commons
Surrey

Boscastle
Cornwall

Box & Leith Hills
Surrey

Braithwaite Hall
Yorkshire Dales

Brancaster Millenium Activity Centre
Norfolk

Brimham Rocks
Yorkshire

Brockhampton Estate
Herefordshire

Canons Ashby
Northamptonshire

Carnewas & Bedruthan Steps
Cornwall

Castle Drogo
Devon

Castle Ward House & Demesne
Co. Down, Northern Ireland

Chartwell
Kent

Chiltern Gateway Centre, Dunstable Downs
Bedfordshire

Chirk Castle
Wrexham

Clandon Park
Surrey

Claydon
Buckinghamshire

Cleddau Woodlands
Pembrokeshire

Cliveden
Berkshire

Clumber Park
Nottinghamshire

Colby Woodland Garden
Pembrokeshire

Cotehele
Cornwall

Craflwyn & Beddgelert (Snowdonia)
Gwynedd

Cragside
Northumberland

Croome
Worcestershire

Cuckmere Valley
Sussex

Denbies Hillside
Surrey

Devils Dyke
Sussex

Dinefwyr Park and Castle
Carmarthenshire

Downhill Demesne
Co. Londonderry, Northern Ireland

Downs Banks
Staffordshire

Dudmaston
Shropshire

Dunham Massey
Cheshire

East Riddlesden Hall
Yorkshire

Erddig
Wrexham

Felbrigg Hall
Norfolk

Finch Foundry
Devon

Florence Court
Co. Fermanagh, Northern Ireland

Formby
Liverpool

Fountains Abbey and Studley Royal
Yorkshire

Fowey Estuary
Cornwall

Fyne Court
Somerset

Gibside
Tyne & Wear

Gower: Rhossili
Swansea

Grasmere
Cumbria

Greys Court
Oxfordshire

Hardcastle Crags
Yorkshire

Hatchlands Park
Surrey

Hatfield Forest
Essex

Hawkshead and Claife
Cumbria

Headley Heath
Surrey

Heysham Head
Morecombe Bay, Lancashire

Hezlett House
Co. Londonderry, Northern Ireland

Hughenden
Buckinghamshire

Ilam Park
Derbyshire

Killerton
Devon

Kingston Lacy
Dorset

Knole
Kent

Lacock Abbey
Wiltshire

Lanhydrock
Cornwall

Lantic Bay & Lansallos
Cornwall

Leigh Woods
Bristol

Lindisfarne
Northumberland

Looe & Whitsand Bay
Cornwall

Lydford Gorge
Devon

Malham Tarn Estate
Yorkshire Dales

Marloes Peninsula
Pembrokeshire

Marsden Moor
Yorkshire

Morden Hall Park
London

Mottistone Manor
Isle of Wight

Mount Stewart
Co. Down, Northern Ireland

Newton National Nature Reserve
Isle of Wight

North Coast
Co. Londonderry, Northern Ireland

Nostell Priory & Parkland
Yorkshire

Nunnington Hall
Yorkshire

Nymans
Sussex

Osterley Park
London

Oxburgh Hall
Norfolk

Parke
Devon

Pencarrow Head
Cornwall

Penrhyn Castle
Gwynedd

Penshaw Monument
Tyne & Wear

Petworth House and Park
Sussex

Plas Newydd
Anglesey

Plym Valley
Devon

Polperro
West Cornwall

Portstewart Strand
Co. Londonderry, Northern Ireland

Purbeck Countryside
Dorset

Quarry Bank Mill
Cheshire

Rievaulx Terrace
Yorkshire

Rowallane Garden
Co. Down, Northern Ireland

Saltram Devon	**Tintagel Old Post Office** Cornwall
Seaton Delaval Hall Northumberland	**Tredegar House** Newport
Sheringham Park Norfolk	**Trengwainton Garden** Cornwall
Sissinghurst Castle Kent	**Upper Wharfdale** Yorkshire Dales
Sizergh Castle Cumbria	**Waddesdon Manor** Buckinghamshire
Souter Lighthouse Tyne & Wear	**Wallington** Northumberland
St David's Head Pembrokeshire	**Washington Old Hall** Tyne & Wear
Stowe Buckinghamshire	**Watersmeet** Devon
Sutton Hoo Suffolk	**Wicken Fen** Cambridgeshire
Teign Valley Devon	**Wimpole Hall** Cambridgeshire